It's Alive! And Kicking!*

It's Alive!
And Kicking!*

Math the way it ought to be . . . tough, fun . . . and a little weird

by Asa **Kleiman** and David **Washington**
with Mary Ford Washington

Illustrated by Eric Nelson

*Void where prohibited by law

ISBN-13: 978-1-882664-30-6
ISBN-10: 1-882664-30-2

Prufrock Press Inc.
P.O. Box 8813
Waco, TX 76714-8813
(800) 998-2208
http://www.prufrock.com

Contents

Note to teachers:

If some homo non-sapien in your class asks, "May we use calculators?"
Our answer is, "Are mice rodents? Is Asa's sister annoying? Will Jane marry Bob?"
Yes, you can use calculators.

The bold facts in this book are true.
(Everything else is horsefeathers.)

Sources

Andrews, Michael (1977). *The Life that Lives on Man*. Taplinger Publishing: New York.

Conniff, Richard (July 1995). When It Comes to the Pesky Flea, Ignorance is Bliss. *Smithsonian Magazine*, 77-78.

Elfman, Eric (1994). *Almanac of the Gross, Disgusting & Totally Repulsive*. Random House: New York.

Information Please Environmental Almanac (1994). Houghton Mifflin: Boston.

Information Please Almanac, Atlas and Yearbook (1992). Houghton Mifflin: Boston.

Marshfield Wastewater Treatment Center, Marshfield, WI.

Nash, Bartleby (1991*). Mother Nature's Greatest Hits: The Top 40 Wonders of the Animal World*. Living Planet Press: Los Angeles.

National Center for Health Statistics, 1992.

New Grolier's Multimedia Encyclopedia. Grolier Electronic Publishing: Danbury, CT.

Smithsonian Magazine, April 1995.

Thomas, Lewis (1974). *The Lives of a Cell*. Bantam Books: Toronto.

Thomas, Warren, and Kaufman, Daniel (1990*). Dolphin Conferences, Elephant Midwives, and Other Astonishing Facts About Animals*. Tarcher: Los Angeles.

US Department of Agriculture, 1991.

World Health Organization, United Nations, 1990.

Using Really Big Numbers

Big numbers are easy when you remember three things:

☞ each group of three numbers is called a period;

☞ each period has a ones place, a tens place, and hundreds place;

☞ reading from left to right, you say the name of the group at the comma.

Number of commas   Name

Number of commas	Name
1	thousand
2	million
3	billion
4	trillion
5	quadrillion
6	quintillion
7	sextillion
8	septillion
9	octillion
10	nonillion
11	decillion
12	undecillion
13	duodecillion
14	tredecillion
15	quattuordecillion
16	quindecillion
17	sexdecillion
18	septendecillion
19	octodecillion
20	novemdecillion
21	vigintillion
33	googol

So...

1,345,768,095,438 is read
1 trillion, 345 billion, 768 million, 95 thousand, 438

No big deal, right?

There are two million sweat glands in our bodies.

After the last gym class of 35 people, how many sweat glands entered the locker rooms?

Locker room

Mucus moves through our body at the speed of 5 mm per minute.

If you were riding in a tiny mucus-powered bus through your body, how long would it take you to go one meter?

Mucus moves

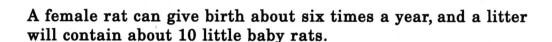

A female rat can give birth about six times a year, and a litter will contain about 10 little baby rats.

Let's say you were imprisoned in a jail cell with one male rat (which you named Manfred) and one female rat (which you named Matilda).

They had babies, and half the babies born the first year were male and half were female. All the baby rats began to reproduce after their first birthday.

How many rats would you have to keep you company by the end of the second year?

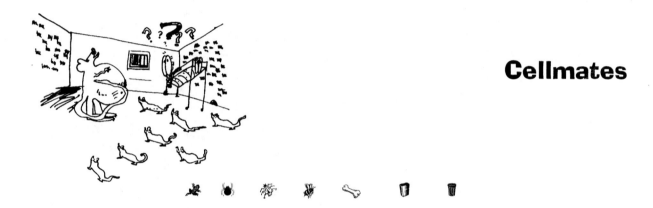

Cellmates

A heavy skin shedder sheds 1½ grams of skin a day, or about 1 pound a year.

If skin scales were selling for 25 cents an ounce, how much could someone like David, who is a pretty heavy shedder, make by selling his skin scales every year? (If you find a buyer please let us know.)

Skin scales
25 cents
a pound

3

During one summer alone a single pair of houseflies, under ideal conditions, can produce as many as 335,923,200,000,000 offspring.

A single pair of houseflies is buzzing around unnoticed, reproducing under ideal conditions.

If it takes Asa 12 swats to kill one fly, how many swats will he need to make to get rid of all the flies produced in one summer?

Swatting ordeal

David's sister is getting her driver's license.

If she hits a mailbox every 2 hours and 15 minutes, what will her grand total be after 18 hours of driving practice?

Mailbox war

Asa has 4 planes hanging from his ceiling. The tacks holding them up are 1 cm long. Each tack is pushed in tightly, however the tacks are beginning to slide at the rate of 1.5 mm per day.

How long until the planes begin their final flight?

**Asa's
airplane**

If David mentions his birthday every day throughout the month of July — once on July 1st, three times on July 2nd, five times on July 3rd, and so on for the entire month — how many times will he mention his birthday on July 30th?

(By the way, his birthday is on July 31st. David says cards and letters may be sent to him at the address printed in the front of the book. Presents will also be accepted. Contact him for gift ideas first.)

**Did I tell you
my birthday?**

While waiting for the dentist, David bit off 5 percent of each fingernail.

His fingernails each used to be 1.2 cm long. How many total millimeters of fingernails did he bite off?

David's dentist appointment

Asa is supposed to floss his teeth using 18" of floss daily. He began a new 50' roll on March 17th.

If he still has 2 feet of floss left after flossing on August 2nd, how many days has he forgotten to floss?

Floss 'em

It is estimated that we inhale nearly 20 billion particles of pollution every day.

David and Asa have determined that the pollution in their town consists of:

☞ 57 percent nasty car odors

☞ 27 percent industrial funky stuff

☞ 18 percent cow manure (hey, they can't help it)

☞ 11 percent sickening cheese factory smell

☞ 8 percent flatulence (human, cow, nematode, etc.)

☞ 4 percent fragrance of gym socks

☞ 3 percent bad breath

☞ 2 percent air fresheners and perfume, and other yuck

What's wrong with their statistics?

Wake up and smell the ...

Humans spray an average of 2.5 saliva droplets into the air with every word they speak.

How many saliva droplets are released into the air every time someone in your math class says, "I don't get it?"

I don't get it

The average person expels 300 saliva droplets per minute while talking.

How many saliva droplets did your teacher expel during the last 50-minute lecture?

Drowning in droplets

There are exactly 2,500,000 rivets in the Eiffel Tower.

If it takes David 1¼ minutes to remove each rivet and 1½ minutes to climb to the next one, how long would it take David to completely de-rivet the Eiffel Tower?

Rivet
number 3

If the cheap person who owes Asa 30 bucks and has given him 3 excuses per day (you know who you are — pay up now!!) will run out of excuses in 7 weeks, how many more excuses can we figure he will come up with?

MY DOG ATE IT

Excuses,
excuses

Asa's grandmother owns a chocolate shop.

Is this relevant?

Relevancy
of chocolate
to mathematics

If 70 percent of refrigerators in the United States contain n.l.r.m.i.t. (no longer recognizable moldy icky things), and 7 out of 8 of these contain more than one n.l.r.m.i.t., what percent of refrigerators contain more than one n.l.r.m.i.t.?

n.l.r.m.i.t.

Mary and David are driving away from a rest stop where David used the restroom and then drank 2 liters of soda. **A full bladder can contain 1.25 liters of fluid, and may fill at the rate of 25 ml per minute.**

If his mom is driving 60 miles per hour and it is a total of 84 miles between rest stops, will David make it to the next restroom before he explodes?

**Stop
the car**

As it turned out, Mary stopped the car by the side of the road, and David quickly ran into the woods. The entire operation only took 54 seconds, during which time he was bitten by 17 mosquitoes per second.

David returned to the car with how many mosquito bites?

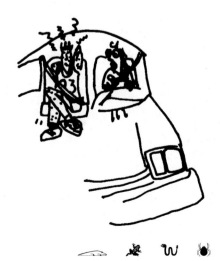

**Let
me in!**

If the population of the Earth continues to increase at the present rate, by 3530 A. D. the total mass of human flesh will equal the weight of the Earth (6.6 sextillion tons), and by 6826 A. D., the total mass of human flesh will equal the mass of the known universe.

If on January 1, 2000, you shaved your head and did not cut it again, and it grew at the rate of 1.5 mm per day, how long would your hair be in the year 3530? 6826? Draw a picture showing approximate length to scale.

A very hairy ordeal

The 25' x 50' septic pool at the wastewater treatment plant contains 157,000 cubic feet of sludge.

If a wastewater sanitation worker fell face first to the bottom of the septic pool, how far would she have to swim to the surface?

Sludge diving

Asa and David were desperately hungry and between them accidentally ate 11 slices of Ms. Washington's whole wheat tofu rutabaga carmel surprise (with 13 tofu chunks per slice).

If Asa ate 39 more chunks than David, how many slices of whole wheat tofu rutabaga carmel surprise did they each eat?

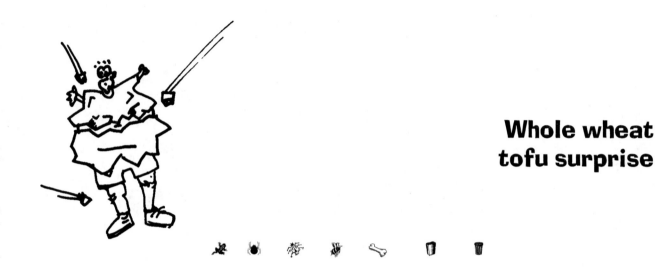

Whole wheat tofu surprise

The average brain weighs three pounds.

After doing this math book, the average brain will weigh about 0.5 pounds more. A post-*It's Alive!* brain is what percent larger than the pre-*It's Alive!* brain?

Heavy thinker

The average mouth produces about 2½ pints of saliva a day.

Asa tried to test this hypothesis, and he did not swallow his saliva at all, but let it all drool into a 4-gallon bucket instead. How long before the bucket was full?

You may wish to try this experiment at home.

(Just kidding.)

Saliva Mouth

A full bladder has a radius of two inches.

Would a full bladder fit into a thermos jug with a circumference of 12"?

What's that in my Thermos?

Waste travels 36" through your colon before it is eliminated.

If it travels the 36" in 3 hours, how many miles per hour is that?

Use fractions if necessary.

**Eliminate
waste**

There are 2½ times as many oil glands on your skin as there are hairs on your body.

If there are 200 million hairs on your body, how many zits will you have if every oil gland suddenly clogs with oil and dirt and breaks forth into a big zit?

**Zit
city**

Ms. Washington is shopping for furniture. Asa and David are helping her (mistake number one).

How much would each of these items cost, adding 5 percent Wisconsin sales tax and $40 delivery fee?

☞ $1,039.99
Genuine 100 percent Cathair Couch — specify tabby or Siamese. (No animals were harmed in the making of this couch.)

☞ $1,995.99
Buick™ back seat — comes in Riviera or Regal, while availability lasts.

☞ $1,412.99
Overstuffed Quicksand Couch — Soft, very soft.

☞ $1,123.58
Giant Whoopee Cushion Bean Bag Chair.

☞ $1,421.06
Prestained Wonder Couch — your choice of catsup, mustard, grease, chocolate, vomit, or ink.

☞ $1,984.00
New for the 90's!!! Lazy Young Person Couch, for the energetically impaired.

☞ $1,043.00
Tissue Paper Couch — for smokers trying to quit.
(or half off with 3,000 Marlboro™ Lung Cancer Miles)

☞ $1,475,380.64
Really Really Really Lazy Boy™ couch, comes with toilet, refrigerator/freezer, microwave, remote control, back up generators, central air and heating. Act now and receive free back scratcher and bottomless chips.

No, we're not
buying a TV

With each breath, we take in about a third of a cubic foot of air. You may be happy to know there are approximately 4 million bacteria in each cubic yard of air.

Inhale. How many bacteria just entered your lungs?

Breathe in

Each person sweats about 1½ pints a day.

How many 8-ounce coffee mugs would this fill?

Coffee, anyone?

Scientists say it is considered quite normal to pass gas 15 times in a 24-hour period (quietly, we hope).

In a 60-minute math class consisting of 28 people including the teacher, how many times could this normally occur?

It's normal

If Asa's temper wears down 2 percent every time his little sister comes to the door and says, "Can I watch?" and she does that once every 30 seconds throughout the day, how long before she ends up stuffed upside down in his clothes hamper?

Asa's temper

At Camp Torture, where David and Asa each spent a few weeks last summer, there was a rule that if you don't finish your lunch, you never eat again. Ever.

Under the bushes out behind the cafeteria/infirmary Friday evening Asa and David discovered the following sandwich remains:

☞ ⅜ egged salad sandwich

☞ ¼ artificial preservative spread on no-wheat whole bleach bread

☞ ⅜ llama milk cheese on Catcher in the Rye bread

☞ ⅝ knuckle sandwich

☞ ⅞ toe-food and toe-mato on hole wheat crisps

☞ ½ Salmon Ella sandwich

☞ ¾ lox and keys on unleveled bread

☞ ¼ Soilent Green Burger Deluxe

When they pieced together all of the sandwich parts, how many total sandwiches had they found?

Camp Torture

David and Asa then threw the sandwiches to Hienz and Gunter, the camp Dobermans, who were distracted by eating the sandwiches (and later by indigestion) long enough to allow David and Asa to slip by unnoticed. When the boys returned, they found that together the dogs had eaten exactly ¼ of a whole sandwich from the remains of each type.

What part of each sandwich was now left?

Heinz and Gunter

If school lunch hotdogs bounce 12 percent of the height from which they fall, how high would one bounce if Asa and David dropped one from:

☞   the top of Asa's garage — 12'?

☞   the top of City Hall — 85'?

☞   a Boeing 747 — 30,000'?

Hot dog

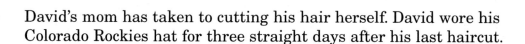

David's mom has taken to cutting his hair herself. David wore his Colorado Rockies hat for three straight days after his last haircut.

The one before, he wore his Mime Radio Fan Club cap for 4½ days straight, and after the haircut before that one, he wore his Camp Torture hat for six straight days.

Is his mom getting better or worse, and how many days will David have to wear his Marshfield Lawn Ornament Society (MLOS) hat after the next haircut?

Let us see your hair, David

A fungus found in Washington state is considered the largest living thing on Earth. It covers 2.5 square miles.

Asa and David are trying to get a cutting of the fungus.

If they can get it to grow that big in their local park, which measures 1½ mile by 1½ mile, how much of the park will be covered?

Fungus

Every second, livestock in the United States excrete 230,000 pounds of manure.

If bacteria did not cause the manure to decompose, and all the cows, sheep, and pigs in the United States kept right on producing the stuff, pretty soon we would be in deep trouble.

How long would it take until the manure produced by American livestock weighed more than the Earth? (The weight of the Earth is 6.6 sextillion tons.)

@#%$!

David's alarm clock is programmed to play the Royal Canadian Bagpipers at 7:08 every morning. If it takes David 9½ minutes to wake up, reach over and push the snooze button, and 23 more minutes before he actually gets out of bed, how long will he have to get ready before it's time to leave for school at 7:45?

Royal
Canadian
bagpipers

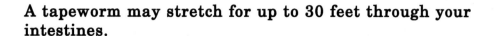

A tapeworm may stretch for up to 30 feet through your intestines.

Assuming it takes 2 feet of tapeworm to tie a bow, would a tapeworm this length be long enough to use to tie up a present which measures 2' in height x 2' in width x 3' in length?

**Oh, what a
pretty bow**

The average person passes about a pint of gas daily.

How long would it take a person to fill a 5,000 gallon hot air balloon with his or her own body gas?

**Up, up,
and away**

Asa and David have determined that on a car windshield measuring 75 cm x 109 cm travelling at 45 miles per hour, junebugs cause the largest splats at 16 square cm, and mosquitoes cause the smallest at 1 square cm. At 45 miles per hour, splats occur every 10 seconds.

☞ At this rate, what is the shortest time it would take for the windshield to totally fill with splats?

☞ Assuming the splats do not overlap, what is the longest time it would take for the total windshield to fill?

Windshield

David's great grandma was ¾ done with her knitting project when David's shoe caught on the yarn. By the time she got his attention, ½ of what she had done had unravelled.

Now how much more does she have to knit?

Great grandma's knitting

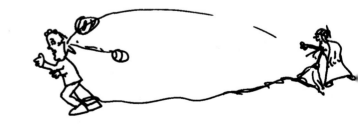

While unsuspectingly watching TV, Asa finds out that the Live and In Concert Oregon Classical Kazoo Symphony Orchestra and Marching Band has come on. It takes him 4 minutes to dig through each box of junk in his room to find his pliers (he uses them to change the channel because his TV has no knobs).

There are 14 boxes of junk in Asa's room. He finally finds his pliers in the last box.

How much of the Oregon Classical Kazoo Symphony Orchestra and Marching Band was he subjected to?

Classical Kazoo Symphony

If David's sister leaves an apple core under her bed and it decomposes into a mass of fuzzy gray mold, losing 4 percent of its original mass each day, what fraction of the *original* apple will be left when David's mom finds it two weeks later?

Fuzzy apple logic

Asa is planning his own talk show, and has made a list of potential guests. He has determined however, that a guest must have one trait from each of the categories below:

Descriptor, Occupation, Hangup

☞ double-jointed goatherders on the Internet
☞ redundant undertakers with redundancy
☞ communist hairstylists and the people who love them
☞ wonderful mathbook publishers who are perfect in every way
☞ ordinary normal people without any problems

How many combinations are possible? Which combination do you like best?

(Unfortunately, as of the date of this publication, Asa has not been able to locate anyone fitting any of the final three categories.)

Live with Asa

A rat can fall 50 feet and land on its feet uninjured.

If David and Asa (accidentally) dropped a rat out of the fifth floor window in a building where each floor is 11 feet high, would the rat survive?

(Editor's note: This is not a nice thing to do.)

A rat can fall 50 feet

Asa and David have a lot of dirty books. In fact, they have both dropped their textbooks on the ground way too many times (and then there was the time David left his out in the rain.)

If ⅚ of the pages in David's books and ⁴⁷⁄₆₈ of the pages in Asa's books are stuck together, which boy will have more trouble finishing his assignments?

Dirty textbooks

Mary censored 12.5 percent of Asa and David's ideas for problems in this book.

How many problems will you never see?

Censorship

Kids should work to save the Earth. Give 49 uses for your old math textbook.

☞ Use them as bricks to make homes for the homeless.

☞

☞

☞

☞

49 uses

Are all things which are weird also disgusting? Are all disgusting things gross?

Create a Venn Diagram showing the relationship between weird, gross, disgusting, and abnormal.

Be able to justify your answer with specific examples. No using names of people.

Gross
and disgusting

Mary, David, and Asa went to this restaurant to eat. How much did Mary pay for the three of them?

Asa's order:
Macaroni and Sneeze
Large Classic Choke with cup
Rhubarb Wire Pie — 4 feet.

David's order:
Thinsulate Pancakes
Large Arti Choke with cup
Last Stand Custard.

Mary's order:
Deep fried lint with French Flies
Large Dr. Kevorkian (no cup)
Hot Sludge Sundae

AFTERMATH RESTAURANT MENU

Entrees:

Macaroni and Sneeze	$5.20
Pseudo-chicken Parts in white whine sauce	$4.25
Deep Fried Lint (please specify dryer or pocket)	$7.28
Thinsulate Pancakes in clogged cabin syrup	$4.68
Wax fruit bowl delicately scented with smelly markers	$6.21
Dead things a la rice — make an offer (rice extra)	
Racial Slurs with a side of aggression	$6.66
Or try Our Value Meal:: Xeroxed foods	$10 cents per sheet
any order with French Flies	add $.50

Beverages*   small $.50   medium $.75   large $1.50

Choose from:

Classic Choke, Cherry Choke, Chokecherry, Diet Choke, Arti Choke, Die-t Dr. Kevorkian, or pure caffeine

*with cups add an additional $1.00

Desserts:

Last Stand Custard	$3.25
Baked Alaska (actual chunks included)	$4.95
Ice Scream	$ 2.25
Rhubarb Wire Pie.	$2 per foot
Sweep-potato Pie	$ 2.55
Hot Sludge Sundae	$2.60
	add 5 percent sales tax

❀ Eat at your own risk ❀
The management accepts no responsibility
for health of its customers.

Care to join us?

Answer Key

Warning: answers may vary due to rounding.
That's cool.

Locker room

35 people x 2 million = **70 million sweat glands**

Mucus moves

1 meter = 1000 mm

1,000 mm ÷5 mm/min = 200 min

200 min ÷60 min/hr = 3⅓ hr = **3 hours 20 minutes**

Cellmates

Step #1)
Start with 2 original rats, Manfred and Matilda.

Step #2)
Manfred and Matilda reproduce.
Give birth 6 times in first year x 10 rats/litter = 60 baby rats

Step # 3)
Manfred and Matilda reproduce second year.
Give birth 6 times in the 2nd year x 10 rats/litter = 60 more rats

Step # 4)
Meanwhile, the 60 rats born in the first year also give birth.
30 pairs x 60 babies = 1,800 new rats

Total: 2 + 60 + 60+ 1,800 = **1,922 rat friends**

Skin scales 25 cents a pound. (Do I hear 30?)

16 ounces = 1 pound

16 x $.25 per ounce = **$4.00 per year**

Swatting ordeal

335,923,200,000,000 offspring x 12 swats per baby = 4,031,078,400,000,000 swats

+ 24 swats for original flies who caused the overpopulation problem in the first place = **4,031,078,400,000,024 swats**

Mailbox war

18 hours driving ÷ 2¼ hours = **8 mailboxes**

Asa's airplanes: final flight

1 cm long ÷ 1.5 mm per day=

10 mm ÷1.5 mm per day = 6.6666 = **6⅔ days (or for the more precise among you) 6 days, 16 hours**

Did I tell you my birthday is July 31st?

Construct a chart, then look for a pattern:

July 1st — 1 time

July 2nd — 3 times

July 3rd — 5 times

An astute mathematical wizard like yourself should be able to see that David mentions his birthday 2 times the date minus 1.

Use this formula (2d-1) to determine the number on July 30th.

2(30) - 1 = **59 times**

So you want extra credit, do you? How many times did David mention his birthday throughout the month of July, up to and including July 31st?
Find a formula.

David's dentist appointment

1.2 cm x 10 fingers x 10 mm/cm = 120 mm to start

120 mm x .05 = **6 mm total fingernails he bit off**

Floss 'em

March 17th - August 2nd = how many days he flossed

15 days Mar + 30 Apr + 31 May + 30 June + 31 July + 2 Aug = 139 total days

50' roll on - 2 feet of floss left = 48' used

48 ft ÷ 1½ ft/day = 32 days he flossed

139 days - 32 days = **107 days he forgot**

Wake up and smell the ...

It adds up to 130%. Anything more than 100% is wrong.

I don't get it

2.5 saliva droplets/word x 4 words = **10 saliva droplets**

Drowning in droplets

300 saliva droplets x 50 minutes = **15,000 saliva droplets**

Rivet number three, rivet number four ...

1¼ minutes to remove + ½ minutes to climb = 2.75 min/rivet

2,500,000 x 2.75 = 6,875,000 minutes

6,875,000 min ÷ 60 min/hr = 114583.33 hr = 114583 hr 20 min

114583 hr ÷ 24 hr/day = 4774.2916 days = 4774.2916 days ÷365.25 days/yr = 13.071298 years

It would take him approximately 13 years.

Excuses, excuses

7 weeks x 7 days/wk = 49 days

3 excuses per day x 49 days = **147 excuses**

The relevancy of chocolate to mathematics

The sum of the chocolate is the square root of the transverse reality colon of the integer choc minus the negative prime-late intruded with the partial composite o, divided exportionately by the sum total of chocolate lovers in the United States, leading one to believe that the authors are slightly crazy, a somewhat warranted assumption, true also for the vast majority of the global populace.

n.l.r.m.i.t.

70% contain n.l.r.m.i.t.

7 out of 8 of these contain more than one n.l.r.m.i.t

What percent of refrigerators contain more than one n.l.r.m.i.t.?

7 out of 8 = ⅞ = 7÷8 = 0.875 (which is 87½%)

To find part of something, multiply the part times the something.

0.875 x .70 = 0.6125 =

61¼% have more than one n.l.r.m.i.t.

Stop the car

84 mi ÷60 mi/hr = 1.4 hr

1.4 hr x 60 min/hr = 84 min

1.25 liters = 1,250 ml in bladder when full

84 min x 25 ml/min = 2,100 ml at end of 84 min

Conclusion: David's mom better stop.

Let me in!

54 sec x 17 mosquitoes/sec = **918 mosquito bites**

A very hairy ordeal

This problem is time consuming, and we're tired. If you figure it out, great. Send us the answer. We'll send you a lock of hair.

Sludge diving

length x width x depth = volume

25 ft x 50 ft x depth = 157,000 cu ft

1,250 x depth = 157,000 cu ft

157,000 cu ft ÷ 1,250 = **125.6 feet to the surface**

Whole wheat tofu rutabaga caramel surprise

39 chunks ÷ 13 chunks/slice = Asa ate 3 slices more than David

We know 11 - 3 = 8, and 8 ÷ 2 = 4, so we know **David ate 4, and Asa ate 7**.

Heavy thinker

3 pounds / 3.5 pounds

It gained 0.5 pounds.

0.5 pounds compared to 3 pounds is 0.5 ÷ 3.0 = 0.166666

Your brain increased approximately 17% in size.

Saliva mouth

2 pts/qt x 4 qt/gal = 8 pt/gal

8 pt/gal x 4 gal/bucket = 32 pt/bucket

32 pt/bucket ÷ 2½ pints/day = **12.8 days**

12.8 days = 12 days + 0.8 day = 0.8 day x 24 hr/day = 19.2 hours

0.2 hr x 60 min/hr = 12 minutes or **12 days, 19 hours, 12 minutes**

What's that in my thermos?

Radius is always half the diameter.

Circumference is always about 3 times the diameter.

There's a formula to figure it more exactly:

π x diameter = circumference

π = 3.14

3.14 x (2 x 2) = 12.56"

No.

Eliminate waste

36" in 3 hours

12" in 1 hour

12" = 1 foot

5,280 feet = 1 mile

1/5280 mi/hr

Zit city

200 million hairs x 2.5 oil glands/hair = **500 million oil glands**

No, we are not buying a widescreen TV

For each price multiply x 0.05 (Wisconsin sales tax), then add the $40 delivery fee

☞ Genuine 100% Cathair Couch
1,039.99 x 0.05 = $51.9995 = $52.00
1,039.99 + $52.00 + $40 = **$1,131.99**

☞ Buick back seat
1,995.99 x 0.05 = 99.7995 = 99.80
1,995.99 + 99.80 + 40 = **$2,135.19**

☞ Overstuffed Quicksand Couch
1,412.99 x 0.05 = 70.6495 = 70.65
1,412.99 + 70.65 + 40 = **$1,523.64**

☞ Whoopee Cushion Bean Bag Chair
1,123.58 x 0.05 = 56.179
1,123.58 + 56.18 + 40 = $1,219.76

☞ Prestained Wonder Couch
1,421.06 x 0.05 = 71.053
1,421.06 + 71.05 + 40 = **$1,532.11**

☞ Lazy Young Person Couch
1,984.00 x 0.05 = 99.20
1,984.00 + 99.20 + 40 = **$2,123.20**

☞ Tissue Paper Couch
1,043.00 x 0.05 = 52.15
1,043.00 + 52.15 + 40 = **$1,135.15**

☞ Really Really Really Lazy Boy
1,475,380.64 x 0.05 = 73,769.03
1,475,380.64 + 73,769.03 + 40 = **$1,549,189.64**

Breathe in.

4 million bacteria/cubic yard of air

3 feet = 1 yard   1 cubic yard = 3 x 3 x 3 = 27 cubic feet

4,000,000 bacteria/cubic yard ÷ 27 cubic feet/cubic yard = 148,148 bacteria/cubic foot

⅓ cubic foot x 148,148 bacteria = **49,383 bacteria**

Coffee anyone?

8 ounces = 1 cup = 1 mug

1 pint = 2 mugs

1½ pints = **3 mugs**

It's normal

15 times/day x 28 people = 420 times/day

420 times/day ÷ 24 hours/day = **17.5 times/hour**

Asa's temper

Wears down 2% every ½ minute, so 4% every minute.

100% ÷ 4%/minute = **In exactly 25 minutes**

Camp Torture

⅜ = ⅜ egged salad sandwich
¼ = ²⁄₈ artificial preservative spread
⅜ = ⅜ llama milk cheese on Catcher in the Rye bread
⅝ = ⅝ knuckle sandwich
⅞ = ⅞ toe-food and toe-mato on hole wheat crisps
½ = ⁴⁄₈ Salmon Ella sandwich
¾ = ⁶⁄₈ lox and keys on unleveled bread
¼ = ²⁄₈ Soilent Green Burger Deluxe

³²⁄₈ = **4 whole sandwiches**

Hienz and Gunter

⅜ - ²⁄₈ = ⅛ egged salad sandwich

¼ - ¼ = **0** artificial preservative spread

⅜ - ²⁄₈ = ⅛ llama milk cheese on Catcher in the Rye bread

⅝ - ²⁄₈ = ⅜ knuckle sandwich

⅞ - ²⁄₈ = ⅝ toe-food and toe-mato on hole wheat crisps

½ - ¼ = ¼ Salmon Ella sandwich

¾ - ¼ = ½ lox and keys on unleveled bread

¼ - ¼ = **0** Soilent Green Burger Deluxe

Hot dog

☞ the top of Asa's garage
    12' x 0.12 = **1.44 feet**

☞ the top of City Hall
    85' x 0.12 = **10.2 feet**

☞ a Boeing 747
    30,000' x 0.12 = **3,600 feet**

Let us see your hair, David

last haircut Colorado Rockies hat — 3 days

one before Mime Radio Fan Club cap — 4½ days straight

before that one Camp Torture hat — 6 days

Fortunately, his mom must be improving (or else David is getting used
to funny hair) and at this rate he will only have to wear his
Marshfield Lawn Ornament Society hat 1½ days

(subtract 1½ days each time)

Fungus

Area = length x width

Use fractions:

1½ x 1½ = ³⁄₂ x ³⁄₂ = ⁹⁄₄ = 2¼ sq mi

Or use decimals:

1.5 x 1.5 = 2.25 sq mi

Either way, the whole park would be covered.

@#%$!

230,000 pounds of manure/second
230,000÷2000 = 115 tons/second

6.6 sextillion tons ÷115 tons/second = 0.05739130435 sextillion sec

Sextillion has 21 zeroes, so move decimal point 21 places

57,391,304,350,000,000,000 seconds will not fit on most calculators so:
57,391,304,350 billion sec ÷ 60 sec/min = 956,521,739,170,000,000 min
956,521,739,170,000,000 min ÷ 60 min/hr = 15,942,028.986 billion hr
15,942,028,986,000,000 hr ÷ 24 hr/day = 664,251,207,750,000 days
664,251,207,750,000 days ÷ 365.25 days/yr = **1,818,620,692,000 years**

EDITOR'S NOTE: When we checked this with a math professor at Baylor University, he noted that any answer that has approximately 1.81 or 1.82 trillion years would be considered correct because we cannot expect more than three significant digits. This is due to the fact that the original data have no more than three significant digits. He also said math sounds like it has gotten harder since he was in school!

Royal Canadian Bagpipers

7:08 am

9½ min + 23 min
7:40½ when he finally gets out of bed

7:45 a.m. - 7:40½ = **4½ minutes to get ready**

Oh, what a pretty bow!

2' in height x 2' width x 3' in length

We better draw this one.

To tie a present we go around the circumference each way.

One ribbon will begin at the middle of the top, stretch across

1.5', then down 2', then across 3', then up 2', then across 1.5'.

Another ribbon will begin at the middle of the top, and stretch across

1', then down 2', then across 2', then up 2', then back 1'.

Add up these lengths and you get:

[1.5 + 2 + 3 + 2 + 1.5] + [1 + 2 + 2 + 2 + 1] = 18 feet

18' + 2' for bow = 20' **yes, it would be enough**

Up, up, and away!

We know that 2 pints = 1 quart, and 4 quarts = 1 gallon, so 1 pint = ⅛ gallon.

5,000 gallons x 8 = 40,000 days

40,000 ÷ 365.25 days/yr = **109.51403 yr or about 109½ years**

Windshield

☞   Junebugs would take the shortest time to fill up the windshield.

The windshield is 75 cm x 109 cm = 8,175 sq cm

8,175 sq cm ÷ 16 sq cm/junebug = 510.9375 junebugs needed

511 junebugs x 10 seconds each = 5,110 seconds

5,110 sec ÷ 60 sec/min = 85.17 minutes =

85.17 minutes ÷ 60 min/hr = **about 1.4 hours**

☞   Mosquitoes would take the longest.

8,175 sq cm ÷ 1 sq cm/mosquito = 8,175 mosquitoes needed

8,175 mosquitoes x 10 sec each = 81,750 sec

81,750 sec ÷ 60 sec/min = 1,362.5 min

1,362.5 min ÷ 60 min/hr = **622.71 hours**

Great grandma's knitting

½ of what she had done became unravelled

She had done ¾

½ x ¾ = ⅜ of finished project became unravelled but ⅜ of the finished project is still intact

1 - ⅜ = **⅝ more to do**

Classical Kazoo Symphony Orchestra

4 minutes x 14 boxes of junk = **56 minutes**

Fuzzy apple logic

0.04 x 14 days = 0.56 = 56% of its mass it has lost

100% - 56% = **44% of its original mass is left**

Live with Asa!!

We have 5 possibilities from each list from which to choose. We may use each choice more than once. There are no other stipulations. Therefore,

5 x 5 x 5 = **125 possibilities**

A rat can fall 50 feet and land on its feet uninjured

We can assume that if they were leaning out a window on the fifth floor, they were actually closer to the top of the fourth story (the floor beneath their feet), than they were to the top of the fifth story (the ceiling above their heads). Even assuming the point where they released the rat was halfway between the floor and the ceiling, we would find

11 feet x 4.5 high = 49.5 feet

The rat would survive

Dirty textbooks

An easy way to figure this one out is to remember that fractions are just decimals waiting to happen (and vice versa).

³⁄₇ of the pages in David's books = 3 ÷ 7 = 0.4285714 = 43%

⁴⁷⁄₆₈ of the pages in Asa's books = 47 ÷ 68 = 0.6911764 = 69%

Asa will be in even worse trouble.

Censorship!

If P = total number of problems before censoring, then 87.5% x P = 52

0.875 x P = 52

52 ÷ 0.875 = 59.42

P - 52 = number of censored problems

59 - 52 = **7 censored problems**

49 uses

The possibilities are endless:

1) use them as bricks to make homes for the homeless.
2) repave your sidewalk with them
3) use them to support your tomato plants
4) develop a new sport - book skiing
5) use them as arm lifts
6) actually do the problems in them
7) build a partition in your room
8) feed them to goats
9) bury them in a time capsule
10) time how fast they drop from the top of City Hall
11) grind them up in the blender to make paper to make more math books
12) eat them
13) shred them and use the shreds to fill your mattress
14) teach someone math

Gross and Disgusting

There are only two correct possibilities here:

1) **yours should look exactly like ours in every way, shape and detail**
2) **it may be different**

Some things to consider:
- The temperature on Friday may be above normal (abnormal), but that in itself might not be weird. We are all used to fluctuations in the weather.
- Can something be disgusting and still be normal? Most definitely.
- Are all things gross also disgusting? Perhaps. Have you ever seen a dissected cow eye? It's incredibly gross, but not really disgusting.
- Are all things which are disgusting things also gross? No. Cheating is not gross in any way, but it certainly is disgusting. (By the way, just why are you looking in the answer key anyhow?)

Care to Join Us?

Asa's order:
Macaroni and Sneeze — $5.20 + Large Classic Choke with cup — $2.50 + Rhubarb wire pie - 4 feet. — $8.00

David's order:
Thinsulate Pancakes — $4.68 + Large Arti Choke with cup — $2.50 + Last Stand Custard — $3.25

Mary's order:
Deep fried lint with French Flies — $7.28 + 0.50 + Large Dr. Kevorkian (no cup) — $1.50 + Hot Sludge Sundae — $2.60

subtotal $38.01

$38.01 x 0.05 =$1.90

$ 38.01 subtotal + 1.90 sales tax = **$39.91 total bill**

About the Authors

Asa and David are two computer geeks who are hopeless misfits and have no lives whatsoever. After doing this book, you will come to see why.

Asa Kleiman has gone completely insane, but hides it relatively well.

David Washington is normal in comparison, which doesn't count for much. He admits he can be extremely annoying, but he denies the frog incident entirely.

Denial

Mary feels bad that this book is not always nice to girls, but it is also not always nice to boys, and Asa and David say if you want to write a math book that's nicer to girls, go ahead.

Special Thanks

We owe anywhere from begrudging thanks to undying gratitude to the following people. We'll let them figure out which.

Dana
Taco Bell
Mom, Dad
Hormel Foods
Monty Python
Prufrock Press
Blue Bunny Popsicles
the guy in the trench coat
Grandma and Grandpa Ford
Scotty Shaw, proofreader, 5th grade
Carrie, Carmen, and Esther Washington
Marshfield Public Library Research Librarian